Mountain to Desert
Building the HO scale Daneville & Donner River

By Pelle K. Søeborg

Presented by

Keith and Kathleen Kauffmann

In Memory of

Carlysle Pemberton, Jr.

Downers Grove
Public Library

KALMBACH
BOOKS

Printed in the United States of America

10 09 08 07 06   1 2 3 4 5

Visit our Web site at
kalmbachbooks.com
Secure online ordering available

Publisher's Cataloging-In-Publication Data
(Prepared by The Donohue Group, Inc.)

Søeborg, Pelle K.
    Mountain to desert : building the HO scale Daneville & Donner River / by Pelle K. Søeborg.

    p.: ill. ; cm.

    Includes index.
    ISBN-13: 978-0-89024-675-7
    ISBN-10: 0-89024-675-0

1. Railroads--Models.   2. Railroads--Models--Design and construction--Handbooks, manuals, etc.   3. Railroad bridges--Models--Design and construction--Handbooks, manuals, etc.
4. Railroad bridges--Models--Design and construction--Handbooks, manuals, etc. I. Title. II. Title: Building the HO scale Daneville & Donner River

TF197 .S639 2006
625.1/9

Photos: page 4, Claus Løgstrup; all others by Pelle K. Søeborg

Layout and design: Pelle K. Søeborg (www.soeeborg.dk)

Contents

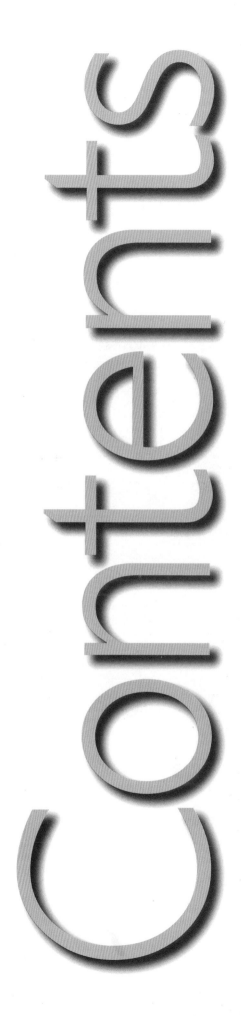

About the Author

Pelle K. Søeborg is a Danish resident and graphic designer. In the early '90s, several *Model Railroader* magazines caught his attention, and he has been a model railroader ever since. A trip to the United States in 1992 added to his interest in modeling U.S. prototypes.

Pelle has written a number of articles for *Model Railroader* magazine throughout the years and has provided photos for model train calendars and for Woodland Scenics and Walthers catalogues.

In addition to model railroading, Pelle enjoys oil painting and photography.

Preface

I have enjoyed trains as long as I can remember. My first train was a Märklin passenger car, which came with a few feet of track. On my 10th birthday, I received a diesel locomotive to pull it. I kept collecting track and trains, but I did not have room for a stationary layout. When I wanted to play with my trains, I laid the track on the floor in my room along with a few Faller and Heljan buildings. Later, as a teenager, I lost interest in my Märklin trains. When I left home and moved into my own place, I sold it all. My love for trains, however, never left me. I still enjoy having to stop my car when I see the crossing gates come down.

One day in the early '90s, I came across some issues of *Model Railroader* magazine in a sale basket at a bookstore in Copenhagen. The realistic scenes on the covers caught my attention. I bought them all and read them over and over. I had never seen modeling like this before, and I was fascinated with the detailing of the featured layouts. The articles about detailing locomotives and building models from scratch also intrigued me.

I decided to take up my childhood hobby again, but this time I wanted to make a North American model railroad. My first attempt was a diorama, but it did not turn out to my satisfaction, and I realized I had to do some research first. That led to my first trip to the U.S. in 1992. It was a great experience to see the Tehachapi Loop, Cajon Pass, and other famous railfan places. The Tehachapi Mountains made a special impression on me. As soon as I returned home, I started building my Tehachapi layout. This layout was later featured in the March 1998 issue of *Model Railroader*.

I moved to a new house in 1999, and sadly, the old layout was torn down. My new home lacked a basement, so I had to settle for a spare bedroom for my trains. The room was not big enough for a layout, so I kept myself busy building a diorama. However, I missed running my trains and ended up building a heated, insulated shed in the garden for the new layout. In fall 2003, the shed was finished, and construction of my new empire, Daneville and Donner River, began.

This book is not meant as a guide for building a model railroad from A to Z. It is a story about what led to the decisions I made on the various issues involved in building a model railroad, with helpful hints based on the many questions I have been asked as a result of my articles in *Model Railroader* magazine.

I hope the book will be an inspiration to those of you who are building your first model railroad, as well as to those of you building your next layout.

Introduction

The West, that characteristically and uniquely American landscape, is where nature reveals its extremes, from the heat of below-sea-level deserts to the cold of breathtakingly tall peaks. American railroaders fought the land, the native peoples, and each other in their struggles to build the great transcontinental lines. Today, those builders have become legends. The names of those railroads – Santa Fe and Union Pacific, among others – still evoke dramatic images, and their successors still struggle to move freight across the unforgiving landscape.

Given all that, you can imagine the surprise of *Model Railroader's* readers when they learn that one of today's leading modelers of the West is a Dane, not an American, or that his layout, which looks so expansive in photos, is actually a mid-sized layout. Even those of us who have the pleasure of knowing Pelle Søeborg continue to be amazed at not only his creativity and his talent, but also his ability to create a model environment that simply looks right.

Translating real locations, especially Western locations, into model form is not the simple task that it might appear to be. It takes a blend of research skill, artistic sensibility, and modeling acumen to build a layout in which the trains and the landscape complement each other. One of the keys to making this happen is actually practicing restraint. The real landscapes may appear larger than life, but what works in the wide-open spaces doesn't always work well in a model-railroad-sized space. Pelle understands that fact, and he used that knowledge when planning and building his model railroad.

Pelle has all the skills needed to create a realistic layout; he's a painstaking researcher, a terrific builder, and a gifted artist. Happily for those of us who are model railroaders, he's also an extremely talented photographer and a patient teacher. His articles have entertained, encouraged, and educated hundreds of thousands of MR readers over the years. Now, in this book, he tells the story of his newest railroad, including how he designed it and the techniques he used to build it. I think you'll find it enjoyable, inspirational, and useful; I know I did.

Terry Thompson, Editor
Model Railroader

Daneville

Have you ever heard of Daneville, California? No? Then let me take you on a guided railfan tour of this Western dream town. In Daneville, the sun always shines and you will find plenty of action. The Union Pacific Railroad's main line runs right through town, and the Burlington Northern Santa Fe has trackage rights. The town itself offers plenty of hotels and places to eat. If you need gasoline, you can fill up your car at the ARCO gas station, which also features an *ampm* market stocked with water, snacks, and other supplies for the road.

If you are looking for a burger, you will find a McDonald's at the east end of Daneville. Another place, JR. Market, offers cool drinks and more.

Pay attention to the speed limits in Daneville because there is a good chance speeders will be pulled over by the highway patrol.

During my trips, I found railroad areas that fascinated me and inspired my layout design. My approach to modeling is more of a railfan than an operator. You could say that I try to re-create the flavor of a region.

Daneville, as I named the town on my layout, might look familiar to you, and there is a good reason for that. Most of the buildings on the main street of Daneville can be found in Mojave, Calif. To me, Mojave is a typical Western railroad town. The tracks run alongside the main street, and there are plenty of hotels and restaurants. Mojave was ideal for my HO scale railroad town.

Still, my town and layout show flexibility. When re-creating an area in 1:87 scale, I "paint" it the way I like. In other words, I am not doing an exact replica of an area but am trying to capture the flavor of an area. That goes for Daneville too.

My billboards are scratchbuilt from Evergreen styrene parts. The signs are a mix of photos of real billboards and prints found in magazines. The displays are attached to the pole with double-sided tape, which makes them easy to replace.

Perry, who lives on Walnut Street on the outskirts of Daneville, is an avid railfan, and the tracks are not far from his house.

Heading west, take a left turn at Western Avenue, and you will reach Daneville Road. Before chasing trains in the desert, it might be a good idea to fill your gas tank at the ARCO station. You won't find many gas stations out there.

The buildings in Daneville

Whenever possible, I use commercial plastic or wood kits for my buildings, but in some cases, no practical kits are available. I could not find any commercial kits of modern business district buildings, so I decided to build them from scratch. On a trip to California, I photographed the structures I wanted to build for my layout.

Several of the buildings, like the Denny's restaurant, hold special meaning for me. On my very first trip to the United States, my first stop for breakfast was at Denny's in Mojave. I found myself at a table by the window with a view of the tracks. While waiting for my Grand Slam, I watched a sparkling new set of warbonnets pass by, pulling an endless string of trailers on flatcars. I could not have had a better introduction to American railroading. Ever since, many more railfan adventures have started with breakfast at that Denny's in Mojave.

I have also filled my car and bought cold soft drinks at the ARCO gas station many times. Mojave has a special place in my heart, and there was no doubt that Mojave would have a place on my layout.

I did not compress the dimensions of the buildings, but they are all backdrop structures, which means that I only modeled one-third of the buildings' depth. That saves space, and you still have a pretty good illusion of a town.

The structures are made from styrene sheets and assorted styrene strips. The roofs consist of various tile-patterned styrene sheets or American Model Builders peel-and-stick shingles on plain styrene sheets.

Most of the parts were cut on a computer-controlled milling machine, which makes scratchbuilding a lot faster and more exact. I made scale drawings of the buildings using my photos as references. I did not measure the actual buildings in Mojave.

Daneville offers everything a railfan could dream of. If you wish to stay overnight, you have several options. The Best Value Inn at one end of town offers nice rooms at moderate rates. If you require more comfort, the Best Western Desert Winds is a good choice. Both hotels have rooms with views of the tracks. I recommend getting a bite at Denny's or one of the other fine restaurants in Daneville before leaving town.

Instead, I used a door as a reference to estimate the dimensions of each structure. Before painting the assembled buildings, I gave them a coat of clear lacquer and sprinkled Arizona Rock & Mineral Roof Sand over the wet lacquer. This sand simulates the stucco found on many modern buildings. When the surface was dry, I blew off the loose sand and painted the buildings in their respective colors.

In most cases, the signs were photos of real signs that I printed on self-adhesive paper using a laser printer. Sometimes, I created new artwork using Adobe Illustrator on my computer.

Not all buildings in Daneville are built from scratch. The depot is a laser kit from American Model Builders, which I bought because I like old wooden depot buildings. My excuse for placing it on my modern-era layout was that I needed a building for the local railroad office and storage for the maintenance crew.

The railroad-served businesses in Daneville are also commercial kits. The lumberyard and plastic pellet transfer are from Walthers, and the warehouse is a Great West Models kit.

I usually make small improvements to the kits. In Daneville, I put better-looking railings and walkways on the plastic pellet transfer and added rooftop details to the warehouse.

Modeling the present time period is a challenge. For example, after I finished the Denny's restaurant, the company changed its corporate design. The prototype restaurant now has gray walls instead of tan, red trim instead of aqua green, and all new signs. Of course, I had to work in these changes on my Denny's model. If you look closely, you will notice that some photos show Denny's in its old livery, and in others, it appears with the new design.

Most buildings along the main street of Daneville are scratchbuilt. I took photos of the actual buildings in Mojave during a trip to California and then made scale drawings of the buildings. Most of the parts were cut on a computer-controlled milling machine, which makes scratchbuilding a lot faster and more exact. I printed the signs on self-adhesive paper using a laser printer.

Denny's is a popular place with railfans as well as locals. Here, the restaurant sports its new corporate design.

The black Mercedes convertible in the warehouse's parking lot tells us that the boss is in the office today.

At the west end of Daneville Road, where it becomes a dead-end dirt road, there is an old mobile home. I'm not sure if the residents there are railfans.

The grade crossing on Western Avenue is a busy place. You should expect the gates to be down often. This is actually a good place to watch trains. You can pull off the road and park your car at the end of the loading platform near the warehouse. Here, your car won't block the highway or access to the warehouse.

The surroundings

Daneville, like Mojave, is located in the desert. Scenery is of great importance to me. I wanted a landscape with a railroad in it, not a railroad with landscape around it. I left plenty of space around the tracks, and having only an 11' × 22' train room, I do not have a lot of track.

Also, the town itself is pretty spread out, as Western towns usually are. Between the buildings, the open spaces covered with desert soil, weeds, and bushes help give the true feeling of a desert town.

I think model railroads often lack open spaces. In my opinion, many model railroaders tend to put far too much track and too many buildings on their layouts. To me, it is more a matter of what can be left out than what can be crammed in.

I am fascinated with the desert, so I dedicated two-thirds of my layout to a desert scene. I was a little concerned that I couldn't re-create a convincing model of the vast desert landscapes of Southern California in my very limited space. One solution was making a desert backdrop. Also, the fact that much of my layout consists of a single track winding through the scenery adds to the feeling of openness.

Making scenery has become my favorite part of the hobby. Of course, I have lots of photos of my favorite train places to work from, but I rarely use them. The problem with working from photos is that you tend to get too specific, and surprisingly, the real world often does not look realistic in a model. Instead, I try to capture the essence of the area I want to re-create. For example, I noticed that the Mojave Desert is not nearly as flat as one might think. I kept that in mind when I made the basic terrain for my desert scene. The only flat area on my layout is Daneville because my staging is hidden below it.

I create my scenery similar to the way I paint landscapes. I paint a specific landscape but leave out a strange-looking shadow or change a weird-looking branch on a tree. If you don't do these things, the oddities will catch the viewer's eye more than the rest of the scene. The same goes for creating a landscape on a model railroad. Your most important tool is your eyes. If a scene looks wrong to you, you can be sure it will look wrong to everyone else too.

The challenge is to spot any problems. When I made my first diorama, I could see that there was something wrong with the scene but could not figure out what it was. Then I remembered what a friend did. He made ship models, and when he wanted to check the authenticity of his models, he looked at them through a pair of binoculars. That way, he blocked out everything else and focused entirely on his model.

I did not own a pair of binoculars, so I used my camera to take a series of close-ups of my diorama. When I later looked at the slides on a big screen, I had no problem seeing what was wrong in the scenes.

Ever since then, I have checked my scenes using photographs. Actually, it started a hobby within a hobby: taking photos of my layout as if I were an HO-scaled railfan. Sometimes I place my camera on the layout and take pictures from angles I would never be able to see as a operator.

Small surprises can show up on the photos. One day, I placed my camera on the main track pointing toward the lumberyard spur. From the aisle, most of the spur is hidden by buildings. In the photo, there was a dark spot on the track. When I enlarged it on my computer, it turned out to be a small Preiser figure I thought I had lost.

Western Avenue crosses the tracks and leads to two of Daneville's railroad-served businesses. There are no crossing gates here, and you have to watch out for switchers working in the area.

Just before Daneville Road becomes a dirt road, you will find the old Daneville Depot. Daneville hasn't been served by passenger trains for many years, so the depot now serves as an office and storage area for the maintenance crews. The local switcher is also stored here.

Coming to Daneville from the east on Daneville Road, you drive through scenery very typical of the Mojave Desert.

When modeling scenery, especially in areas less than two feet deep, a backdrop, such as my dry, desolate desert scene, helps add depth and realism. On page 33, you can find helpful hints about painting a backdrop.

How to make desert scenery

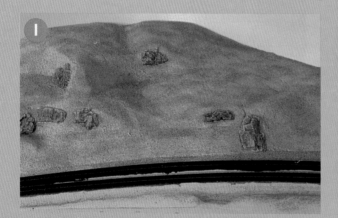

First, I give the terrain a coat of earth-tone water-base paint. While the paint is still wet, I sprinkle on dry sand. The sand leaves a coarse surface that helps prevent the scenery materials from sliding downhill when applied.

After the paint dries, I brush a coat of diluted white glue on the surface. I work on a square-foot section at a time.

I sprinkle Low Desert Soil and Sandstone Rip-Rap from Arizona Rock & Mineral over the area. When the ground is covered, I add Coarse Turf and Underbrush from Woodland Scenics in Burnt Grass and Olive Green.

Finally, I drizzle everything with a mixture of water and rubbing alcohol followed by another drizzle of thinned white glue to set the scene permanently.

The roads

Roads are an important scenic element on my layout. As mentioned earlier, my layout is made from a railfan's point of view. Since roads have taken me to all of my railfan adventures, they occupy a fair amount of space on my layout.

I can see myself driving these roads, looking for the next good photo location while listening to country music on the car radio and feeling the hot desert wind blowing in my face through the open window.

There are a few principles to keep in mind when modeling roads. First, roads tend to follow terrain contours more than railroad tracks because cars can handle steeper grades than trains. It is also easier to build roads around rocks than through them.

Another point to remember when modeling realistic roads is to make sure lane widths are prototypical. It is also a good idea to have smooth gradual curves wherever the road bends.

The choice of pavement material is also an important consideration. I used Woodland Scenics Smooth-It on my roads. It

The road to Daneville parallels the main line and provides excellent opportunities for viewing mixed freight trains.

leaves a realistic surface with a few dips and bulges, just as you find on real roads.

I painted the road surfaces with an asphalt color mixed from Model Master Gull Gray and Sand. I also brush-painted all road striping and markings.

Since my hand is not steady enough to paint the road striping freehand, I marked the outline of the stripes with masking tape. And I cut the left-turn-arrow templates from air-brush masking film.

The roads received some weathering treatment using black chalk powder. I simply dipped my finger in the black powder and used my fingertip to smudge the powder down the center of each lane.

How to make roads

I mark the edges of the road with a pencil and place strips of Woodland Scenics Paving Tape, a self-adhesive foam tape, along the outside edge of the pencil line. My two-lane highways are 25 scale-feet wide. The three-lane main street in Daneville is 35 scale-feet wide.

To model the road surface, I use Woodland Scenics Smooth-It. Smooth-It creates a realistic surface with a few dips and bulges, just as you find on real roads. After the first layer sets but before it dries, I give it a thin second coat to smooth the surface. I add more water to the second mix to make it flow more easily.

When the plaster is completely dry, I lightly sand it. If the sanding reveals some holes in the surface caused by air bubbles, I patch them with some Smooth-It.

I paint the road with a mixture of Model Master Gull Gray and Sand, which gives a warm gray color similar to older sun-bleached asphalt that suits my desert scenery well. I give the road two coats of paint.

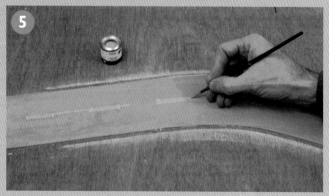

I mask the outline of the stripes with masking tape. All edges are carefully rubbed down to prevent paint from creeping under the tape. Templates for the left-turn arrows found on the main street in Daneville are cut from airbrush masking film. I hand-paint all road stripes and markings this way.

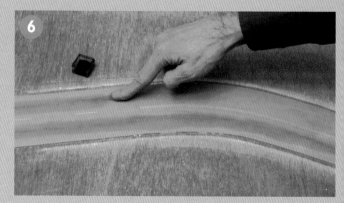

Finally, the roads receive some weathering. Dipping my finger in black chalk powder, I use my fingertip to smudge the powder down the center of each lane.

Along Daneville Road, two businesses are served by rail. The warehouse receives various types of goods from freight cars, mostly boxcars. The plastic pellet transfer silos receive a hopper at least once a week. If you're lucky, you can watch the local freight pick up the freight cars.

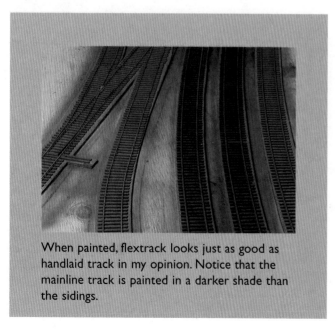

When painted, flextrack looks just as good as handlaid track in my opinion. Notice that the mainline track is painted in a darker shade than the sidings.

The track

Let's not forget that the town buildings and scenery are there because of the railroad. I developed a simple track plan for my railroad. Basically, it is a single track that starts and ends in a hidden staging. A passing siding midway and various spurs to railroad-served businesses provide some operation possibilities.

I planned for 36" curves but had to settle for 33" radius curves. I was afraid my 89-foot-scale auto racks and flat cars would not look good on the 33" curves, but it turned out to be acceptable.

I also compromised on the grades. My steepest grade ended up at 2.6 percent, which was slightly more than the 2.5 percent maximum grade I had planned for.

The old station platform is a perfect place to photograph trains passing through Daneville. The maintenance gang won't hassle you despite the "No trespassing" sign.

Some trains stop at the Daneville depot, which occasionally serves as a crew change point. That gives you plenty of time to take photos of the locomotives.

I used Micro Engineering flextrack on my layout. Micro Engineering makes very nice track that simulates both concrete and wood ties. I chose Micro Engineering track because the cross section of its code 83 rail is slightly narrower than the rail on other track brands, and to me, that looks more realistic.

Unfortunately, Micro Engineering does not make turnouts larger than no. 6, and I wanted longer turnouts for the passing siding at Daneville. For that, I used no. 8 turnouts from Central Valley.

The main line on my layout is all code 83 rail. Sidings are all code 70 except for a code 55 spur track that leads to the lumberyard.

All track on the Daneville subdivision, which is a former Southern Pacific line, has wood ties. The Donner River subdivision, which has always been owned by Union Pacific, has modern track with concrete ties.

How to lay track

1 I cut 17mm-wide roadbed strips from two thicknesses of cork flooring: 7mm for main lines and 4mm for sidings. The strips are attached to the sub-roadbed with white glue, using small nails to hold the alignment on curves.

2 I sand the roadbed surface smooth and lightly sand the edges so there won't be any sharp corners poking out of the ballast. I also sand the transitions between the 7mm and 4mm roadbed.

3 I use my eyes to check if the track is straight and the curves are smooth. The eyes are a very precise instrument for that.

4 I drill holes for spikes in every 15th tie. I only drive the spikes halfway down at first. After checking the track's alignment one last time, I push the spikes all the way down.

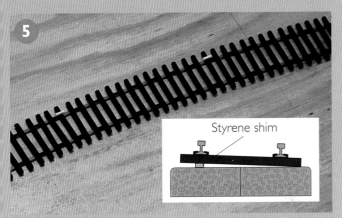

Styrene shim

5 I superelevate my mainline curves by gluing styrene strips to the underside of every 15th tie. For a smooth transition between level and superelevated track, I start with .010" styrene shims at the beginning of the easement, continue with .020" and .030", and end with .040", which is the height of my superelevation.

6 On my main line, I use Central Valley no. 8 turnouts. An advantage of these kits is that they can be curved. Placing them in the easement gives me an extra 20" passing siding length.

Leaving town going east on Daneville Road, you will find Tom's
Place. Tom is not the most organized person in Daneville, but if you
need a fender for an old car or a part for your air conditioner, Tom
is the guy. Tom is also a handyman and very popular among the
locals since he can fix almost anything at a very fair price.

How much detail is enough?

Visitors tend to think that my layout is highly detailed, but I am not a detail freak. I add just enough detail to make a scene look right. How much is enough, you might ask? There is no simple answer, but when you look at a scene and it appears correct, that is enough.

This is my rule of thumb: The closer the scene is to the edge of the layout, the more details I add. Take Tom's Place for example, which is located between the track and the edge of the layout. I scattered all kinds of junk on his property because this is the first scene visitors see when they enter Daneville.

In many cases, only a few details are enough to make a convincing scene: a solitary tree, some old fence posts, a rusty steel barrel laying on the ground, a signpost. Larger details, such as telephone poles, give the layout an authentic feel. I have a lot of telephone poles on my layout to add depth to the scenes.

My telephone poles are from Rix Products. I used the clear crossarms that come in transparent green plastic. Painting them the same color as the pole and leaving the insulators unpainted gives them a realistic look. The wires are from Berkshire Junction, which makes various sizes and colors of elastic string wire.

After crossing the overpass going west, there is an old store that has been out of business for years. Now, squatters have moved in and installed new window glazing and even a stove. Actually, it is a scratchbuilt model of the Caliente Store located in the Tehachapis, one of the few items I used from my earlier layout.

After crossing the overpass going west, you will find the local lumberyard, another of Daneville's railroad-served businesses.

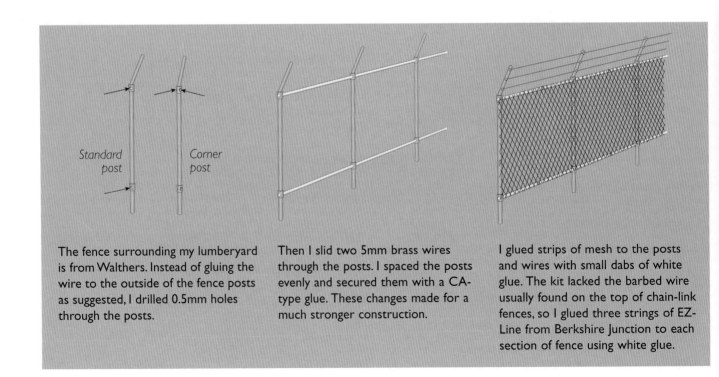

Standard post

Corner post

The fence surrounding my lumberyard is from Walthers. Instead of gluing the wire to the outside of the fence posts as suggested, I drilled 0.5mm holes through the posts.

Then I slid two 5mm brass wires through the posts. I spaced the posts evenly and secured them with a CA-type glue. These changes made for a much stronger construction.

I glued strips of mesh to the posts and wires with small dabs of white glue. The kit lacked the barbed wire usually found on the top of chain-link fences, so I glued three strings of EZ-Line from Berkshire Junction to each section of fence using white glue.

The highway generally follows the track going west out of town, and there are several good photo locations in that area.

Other distinct details include the fence protecting the lumberyard, guardrails, and road signs. I created road signs on my computer, printing them on self-adhesive paper and attaching them to styrene signposts made from thin styrene sheets and T-shaped styrene strips.

Obvious details like railroad signals, relay sheds, and railroad signs are found on my layout. I don't think you have to add zillions of details to your layout to make it appear realistic.

You can add a lot of details if you have the time and patience, but keep in mind that the level of details has to be the same on every part and item on your layout. If you superdetail your locomotives, you also have to do the same to your railroad cars, structures, and scenery. If you don't, the overall appearance of your layout will not look balanced.

Two rusty, old barrels and some weeds next to the depot give it an unused appearance.

A backdrop adds lots of extra miles to a layout, yet I have met many modelers who are convinced they can't paint a nice-looking backdrop. Remember, we are not talking fine art here. You will be surprised by how little effort it takes to create a believable illusion of distance. And no harm is done if it comes out wrong — just start over. Actually, a backdrop is the easiest part of a model railroad layout to change.

There are many ways to paint a backdrop; some modelers even make backdrops using giant photo enlargements. In my case, I decided to use oil colors. I used acrylics on earlier backdrops, but in this layout, I had 60 feet of backdrop to paint and wanted to use a slow-drying paint. The advantage of using oil colors is that you can work with them for hours, even days, depending on the amount of drying additive you use.

Oil colors look fairly glossy when dry. After several months, when the paint was completely dry, I gave the entire backdrop a coat of clear flat finish to kill the shine.

How to paint a backdrop

I start by mixing Ultramarine and white to create six shades of blue ranging from very light, almost white, to deep sky blue. I apply a strip of each shade to the backdrop. I do that on all 60 feet of backdrop.

I blend the strips together with a 2-inch-wide brush. Repeated brush strokes gradually create a smooth transition of color from top to bottom. Completing all 60 feet of sky takes only five hours.

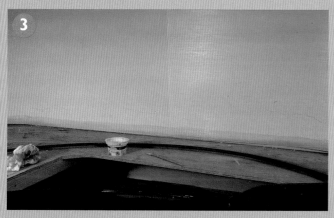

I draw the contours of the landscape with a pencil. I then paint the flat land a desert soil color by mixing Yellow Ochre, Raw Umber, and white, and add more white with a little Ultramarine, working my way from the bottom to the top. The farther away an object is, the more faded and blue it looks.

I make the base color for the mountains from white, Raw Umber, Ultramarine, and a little Yellow Ochre. Ultramarine is important because it gives the illusion of distance. Even though the color does not look blue in the photo, there is quite a bit of Ultramarine in it.

I go over the mountains again, this time with a lighter version of the base color. Finally, I blend the shades together. Desert brush and weeds are dabbed on using a color mixed from Yellow Ochre, Ultramarine, Burnt Umber, and white.

The finished scene nicely illustrates a desert landscape with a mountain ridge in the distance. Even though the scene is no more than 16 inches deep, it gives an illusion of great distance.

West of Daneville, just before the track leaves the highway, you will find Duolith Cement. The only large industry in the area, the plant is an interesting place to visit.

Duolith Cement

The small businesses of Daneville were not able to generate a challenging operating session. A larger industry was needed on the layout. An obvious choice was a cement plant. Due to the limited space available for an industry on my relatively small layout, the size of a railroad yard in connection with the plant would be very limited. Since cement hoppers are short cars, even a small yard can hold several of them.

Originally, I had planned to model my scratchbuilt structure after Monolith Cement, located just outside Tehachapi, Calif. But then Walthers came out with a cement plant. Since scratchbuilding large, complex industrial structures does not really interest me, I decided to use the Walthers kit instead. I added a couple of extra buildings to the complex and a lot of pipes to make it

look more interesting. I have no idea if the pipes can be justified from a cement plant engineer's point of view, but I have noticed lots of pipes on real cement plants, so mine has them too. I also added extra details to the roofs.

I painted the structure in various shades of gray and used powdered pastels to add a little patina to the plant. I must admit that the cement plant is not the structure I am most proud of, but it serves its purpose as being a focal point for operations.

Maybe some day I will replace this cement plant with one that's scratchbuilt, but that project does not have a high priority. It would also not solve what I consider to be a bigger problem: no matter how I model a cement plant, the structure will always seem too small in scale when compared to real cement plants.

A railfan watches the company switcher sorting cement hoppers. He is not trespassing as long as he stays on this side of the main line.

The small yard at the plant can hold up to 10 cement hoppers.

The Narrows

Just before westbound trains leave the Daneville sub and just before they arrive in the hidden staging yard below Daneville, they pass through the Narrows. The landscape here is different from the typical Mojave Desert scenery that covers the rest of the Daneville sub. Inspired by one of my other favorite railroad areas in California, the Tehachapi Mountains, this part of the layout has grass-covered hills. Having hills on this end of the layout also helps disguise the duckunder and the entrance to the staging.

I have spent countless hours in the Tehachapi area over the years, and the grass-covered hills appealed to me from the very first time I saw them. My previous layout was based entirely on the Tehachapi Mountains, and I had to reserve at least a few feet for Tehachapi scenery on this layout too.

This concludes our journey across the Union Pacific's Daneville subdivision. In the following pages, we will embark on a very different trip.

An eastbound UP freight led by C44ACCTE #5739 has just entered the Daneville sub. To get to the Narrows, you have to take the service road, which can be a bumpy ride.

The cows on the hill don't seem to pay any attention to the passing train.

If you climb the hills at the Narrows, you will get a great view of Duolith Cement.

Hundreds of miles north of Daneville, you will find another of my favorite railroading places: Donner River Canyon. While it lacks the comforts of Daneville, with its paved roads, restaurants, and hotels, Donner River Canyon has beautiful scenery. Railfanning the canyon requires some preparation. You will need a four-wheel-drive vehicle, hiking boots, a backpack with food and drinks, and, of course, a camera.

I'll guide you on a tour of Donner River starting at Tunnel 1 and ending near the summit at Tunnel 2. We'll drive to Tunnel 1 via UP's service road. Yes, I know it is trespassing, but nobody has ever said anything to me. The only railroad people I have met here are track inspectors and employees maintaining the signals. Parking our vehicle at Tunnel 1, we'll hike all the way to Tunnel 2. Now put on your hiking boots and let's get started.

One third of my layout represents a mountain area with a single track running along a river. I wanted two completely different types of scenery represented on my layout because creating scenery has become my favorite part of modeling, and making nothing but desert scenery seemed a little monotonous.

Initially, I could not decide if I wanted to use UP's Feather River route or Donner Pass as the inspiration for my mountain. The Feather River features beautiful railroad bridges and a river. The wilderness of Donner Pass has its own beauty. I have camped out with American railfan friends in both places and

like them equally. Here, the advantage of modeling a generic area kicks in – the UP Donner River subdivision was what I had been looking forward to model.

I had never modeled this particular type of mountain scene before. I realized that modeling a mountain is very different from modeling a flat desert. In addition to working with different terrain, I had the opportunity to model tunnels and railroad bridges, which are not often seen in deserts. This area also differs from my desert scene by having no roads except for two service roads leading to the signals at Tunnel 1 and Tunnel 2.

I must admit that I am not very good at reading how-to books before jumping into the actual modeling. I own a few of these books, but it did not cross my mind to see if they contained useful information about modeling mountain scenery. My research basically consisted of what I remembered from my visits to Feather River and Donner Pass and a few photos I took. I had the area laid out in my mind, and I simply worked from that. The photos were mainly used as reference for placing scenery materials onto the terrain.

Service roads

In this rugged terrain, no service roads follow the track all the way. However, signals require access for maintenance, so a road has to lead to them. As in the real world, I had to find the best location for the road using as gentle a grade as possible.

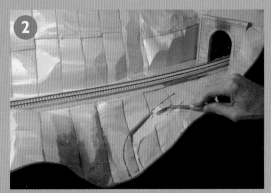

I cut out the road with a foam cutter knife. This illustrates perfectly the advantage of using foam board for terrain. It would not have been easy to do this on terrain fashioned out of chicken wire and plaster.

Finally, I beveled the slopes. Little things like service roads are important in creating realistic scenery.

We don't have to move far from Tunnel 1 before finding the first good photo spot. Just before the track crosses Donner River, we have a great view looking toward Tunnel 1. The track makes a long, sweeping curve toward the bridge. The signals at Tunnel 1 will tell us if a train is approaching, which should give us plenty of time to set up the cameras. I bet we won't have to wait long for an upcoming train to arrive. This is a busy line.

The tunnels

Trains enter and leave this mountain scene through tunnels. Tunnel 1 is the entrance to the hidden staging, and trains travel through Tunnel 2 at the summit to arrive at Daneville. On a model railroad layout, it is a huge advantage to have the track disappear into tunnels to separate different scenes. This is not possible to do in a desert scene.

On my railfan trips, I have often stood outside tunnels wait-

ing for a train to emerge, feeling the excitement as the rumble from deep inside the tunnel gets closer and closer. At last, the engines appear, and huge amounts of black smoke are pulled out by the slipstream. As in real life, tunnels on a model railroad layout add to the drama of mountain railroading.

I have noticed an interesting effect with the tunnels on my layout. My trains are longer than the open track in Donner River Canyon, which means that the train disappears into the second

Tunnel entrances

Using Woodland Scenics Tunnel Liner Form is a quick way to create good-looking tunnel walls. This mold casts rock walls for tunnels, and the shape of the walls match Woodland Scenics tunnel portals. I cast the tunnel-wall sections using Hydrocal. I stained them with diluted Stone Gray, Slate Gray, and black liquid pigments (also by Woodland Scenics). I placed the tunnel-wall sections on the layout and sealed all joints with Flex Paste.

I built up the terrain around the tunnel walls using precut foam blocks, gluing them together with construction glue.

I checked the fit of the tunnel portal and retaining walls. I did not glue them at this point. To avoid damaging or spilling paint on them, it is better to install them after the basic scenery is done.

tunnel before the last car comes out of the first tunnel. In other words, you never see the entire train. A 30-car train appears endless when cars keep coming out of a tunnel long after the locomotives have disappeared into the next tunnel.

Before jumping into the basic terrain, I installed tunnel walls at both ends of the route and made sure there was enough clearance for all types of equipment.

Foam insulation board terrain

While cutting the foam boards, I discovered another way to create terrain. Instead of stacking foam boards on top of each other like a sandwich, I cut profiles and glued them next to each other vertically. This is an easier way to make the rugged shape of a mountain.

It is important to vary the contours of the foam profiles to make more interesting scenery. It also adds more depth to the landscape, giving it a lot of dips and bulges, instead of having a solid wall of rocks along the track. Note how variations in the foam slices give the landscape a more dramatic look.

The terrain

As with my desert scenery, I used foam insulation board for the terrain. Foam insulation board has many advantages. It is strong, easy to work with, and very easy to plant trees in. When working with foam, the shape of the terrain is also easier to see than if you were using chicken wire.

I roughly shaped the basic terrain contours using a hot wire foam cutter. I glued precut foam blocks together using Foam Tack Glue (Woodland Scenics).

While cutting the foam boards, I discovered another way to create terrain. Instead of stacking foam blocks on top of each other like a sandwich, I made profiles and glued them together vertically. An advantage of doing it this way is that it is easier to make the rugged shape of a mountain. I continued the landscape by adding slice after slice of precut foam profiles. I was careful to vary the contours of the profiles to create more dramatic-looking scenery. This method also adds depth to the landscape, giving it a lot of dips and bulges, instead of having a solid wall of rocks along the track. I know that solid walls of rock along a track are found in the real world, but in a model, it does not look right to me.

Another advantage of using foam for the terrain is that it is easy to imagine how the landscape will look, even though it is light blue. The color has prompted visitors to ask if I was doing a winterscape. If they had seen it through my eyes, they would have seen the scenery pretty close to the final result featured on these pages.

The bridges

Railroad bridges always make interesting scenes. On my previous layout, I had a single-section, plate girder bridge where the railroad crossed a road. I loved that scene. There was no doubt that I wanted bridges on this layout as well.

Originally, I planned for two ballasted bridges on the route, but Walthers came out with a nice-looking truss bridge tall enough to handle modern railroad equipment, and I couldn't resist. I imagined the bridge would look terrific carrying the track over the Donner River. But the track was already in place and painted. I had to cut out a section of the plywood roadbed and replace it with the bridge and bridge track.

I assembled and painted the bridge complete with track and weathering before installing it on the layout. I added one item that the kit did not include: a walkway for maintenance people. All modern truss bridges I have seen feature a walkway beside the track.

I installed the painted and weathered bridge abutments and retaining walls and built up the foam terrain around them.

The ballasted plate-girder bridge crosses a small gorge farther up the track. I used parts from a Central Valley kit for my bridge. It is far easier to make a ballasted bridge. I simply glued the bridge sides to the plywood roadbed and scratchbuilt the abutments using styrene sheets.

Opposite page: Looking down at the truss bridge from here gives us an almost head-on shot of the UP locomotive, making for a very dramatic photo.

As soon as the train passes, we can cross the river and relax under the bridge.

Truss bridge

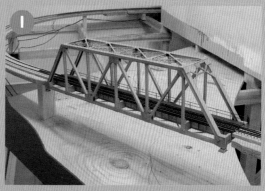

Walthers came out with a nice-looking truss bridge that I couldn't resist. As a result, I cut out a section of the roadbed and concrete track for the originally planned ballasted bridge and replaced it with new bridge track and the truss bridge. I used rail joiners to install the bridge track. After pushing them back flush with the track ends, I placed the bridge in the gap and pulled the rail joiners in place. To make sure there was a reliable electrical connection, I soldered all four joints.

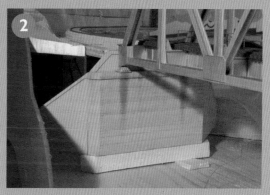

I painted and weathered two bridge abutments (from Walthers) that support the truss bridge. I cut slightly undersized foam supports for the abutments and then fine-tuned their adjustment using small foam wedges.

The riverbank was shaped from foam blocks.

As we get closer to Tunnel 2, we reach a plate girder bridge, which gives us an unobstructed view of trains crossing a gorge.

Ballasted bridge

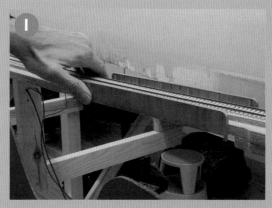

The ballasted bridge was a lot easier to install than the truss bridge. I used two side sections from a Central Valley plate girder bridge kit. I attached the side sections to the plywood sub-roadbed using two-sided foam tape.

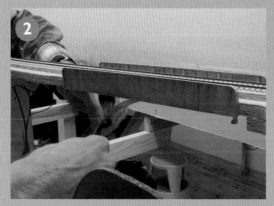

To hide the wood structure, I glued a thin sheet of styrene that was painted gray to the underside of the sub-roadbed.

Then I sealed the side sections to the plywood roadbed with Flex Paste. That served two purposes: it made the attachment stronger, and when ballasting the track, it helped prevent the ballast from falling out between the side sections and the sub-roadbed.

Rock castings and basic scenery

I attached rock castings in various sizes and shapes with construction glue. When more castings were placed close together, I used Hydrocal. Where the wet Hydrocal bulged out between castings, I gently pressed crumpled aluminum foil into it, leaving a surface looking very similar to a rock. Remember to wet the castings before placing them into the wet Hydrocal. If you don't, they will soak up all the moisture from the wet Hydrocal, and your castings won't stick.

To cover the blue foam and make a neutral base color for the scenery products, I gave the terrain a coat of earth-tone water-base paint. I had to be very careful not to get any paint on the rock castings. Next time, I will paint the terrain before applying the rock castings.

In some places, we have to walk near the tracks to avoid climbing steep rocks. We will have plenty of warning if a train comes. You can hear the rumble from the trains long before they come, and they move slowly. The cuts give us several interesting places for taking photos.

Rocks

Rock outcropping adds to the drama of the scenery. To me, a terrain with many rock outcrops of various sizes is more appealing than a solid wall of rock.

I made my castings in the easiest possible way by using various rock molds from Woodland Scenics. The molds I used represented different types of rock, and it is probably not standard practice to mix all of them in the same area. I am not a geologist, so I did not worry about it as long as it looked okay to me.

To disguise the fact that I used many different types of rocks, I stained them all using the same shades of Woodland Scenics Liquid Pigments, so they would appear to be more or less the same type of rock.

I sprinkled sand on the wet paint. This creates an excellent base for the scenery products. The rough surface prevents them from sliding down the hill when applied. Do not work too large an area at a time, or the paint will dry before you have time to apply the sand. I only painted 10- to 15-inch sections at a time.

The next step was to stain the rock castings. I stained them with Woodland Scenics Earth Colors Liquid Pigments. Before staining the castings, I sprayed them with water. Then I dabbed the rocks randomly with diluted Stone Gray, Slate Gray, Raw Umber, and Burnt Umber. Finally, they received a wash of diluted black.

Painting a backdrop

I decided to paint the backdrop before I started applying scenery materials to the terrain. It is easy to spill paint on the scenery when painting, but any stains will be covered by the scenery materials later.

I don't spend much time painting very detailed backdrops. I don't think there is any need to. The backdrop should not be the main attraction on a layout. It is just there to hide the fact that the world ends at a wall. The best result would be if visitors later ask themselves if there had been a backdrop or not.

On my backdrops, one feature I avoid painting is clouds. It is not that difficult to paint clouds, but they always attract attention. When I look at naturalistic paintings of landscapes, I always look at the clouds in the sky because they are so effective. I don't want that to happen on my layout. I want people to look at my scenery and trains – not the backdrop.

Opposite page: It is worth the effort to move a bit away from the track. Hiking down this little canyon will pay off. We can get a dramatic shot of a BNSF SD70MAC.

I must warn you to be careful out here. Look where you place your feet – you could break an ankle – and it is not unusual to see bears in this area.

Backdrop

I used photos of the Feather River area as a reference for this backdrop. The sky was painted in a previous stage, so I started by painting the distant mountains in light blue/green shades. I blended in darker tones for shadows.

The closer hills were painted with more green colors as well as with beige and brown shades. It does not look like it, but there are also blended shades of blue and white in the colors. The hills would look too bright without the blue and white.

Then I painted a zillion pine trees. I did not try to paint exact pine trees. I just dabbed them on using a darker shade of green/blue. Most of the backdrop will be covered later by trees and bushes anyway.

Making the scenery

Using real soil in my desert scenery worked well, so I saw no reason to do anything differently in Donner River Canyon. Arizona Rock & Mineral offers many variations of soil. I chose four different soil colors for my basic mountain scenery, along with different varieties and colors of talus, grass, and turf from Woodland Scenics.

I used real rock ballast from Arizona Rock & Mineral for my track. Because it is heavy, the real rock ballast stays in place when wet.

When I make scenery and things are getting wet – really wet – I cover the floor with newspapers for protection. I punch drain holes in low-lying areas of the terrain, where the water and thinned glue float to, and place containers underneath to collect excess liquid.

I apply all scenery materials, including the ballast, in the same workflow. It saves time and the results look great. The different types of material blend in a more realistic way.

Modeling water

I like seeing the bottom of the river when you look in the water. That is why I picked polyester for my water. I dyed it with a little tan Model Master, being careful to keep it transparent.

I cast 5-6mm layers at a time. It is summer on my layout, and the water level of the Donner River is low. Two layers seemed sufficient.

Trees for Donner River Canyon

The areas I model have substantial numbers of pine trees. I did some research to find out who makes the best-looking pine trees at affordable prices. It was not easy finding realistic-looking model pine trees.

I settled on Woodland Scenics pine trees made with metal-style trunks for two reasons. They keep their shape better than trees with plastic trunks, which have a tendency to return to their original shape after a while. Also, metal trees can be bent into different shapes more easily, while plastic trees have a more uniform look. Since I planned to make more than 150 pine trees, I set up a production line making 10 trees at a time.

If you look back during the climb, you get a spectacular vista of Tunnel 1, the Donner River, and the truss bridge spanning it.

How to make mountain scenery

My choice of soil colors for Donner River Canyon are, from left: Earth, Orange Soil, Cajon Sandstone, and High Desert Soil. These products are all available from Arizona Rock & Mineral. The other cups contain various sizes and colors of talus, and the shakers hold Static Flock Grass, all from Woodland Scenics.

I brush thinned white glue on my work area. Because of the steep hills, I work on just a 1-foot section at a time. When working on an area that is too large, the glue will run down to the bottom of the hills before you can apply the scenery materials.

I place a teaspoon of each of the four shades of soil onto the back of a photo print (any type of stiff cardboard can be used). The four colors are then applied randomly when I gently blew them onto the terrain.

I blow the soil blend prepared earlier onto the wet area, repeating until the entire area is covered. Blow gently. If you blow like the big bad wolf, you can't control where the scenery materials will end up.

I soak the soil with "wet" water, being careful not to wash the scenery materials away. Wet water is water mixed with rubbing alcohol. I use three parts water and one part rubbing alcohol.

I apply small boulders here and there with a spoon. At first, the boulders slid down, but after drizzling them with water, I could push them into place. Once they are wet, they stick to the wet soil.

I cover everything with thinned white glue and then add more soil and some Static Grass Flock. Again, be careful not to wash materials down the slopes.

I sprinkle Static Grass Flock (Harvest Gold and Burnt Grass from Woodland Scenics) on the surrounding hills while they are still wet. Don't worry about adding too much material. When everything is dry, simply vacuum away excess material.

Then I start on the other side of the track. There are no really steep slopes here, so I just spread the soil on the dry surface.

I do not apply the ballast separately. I apply it along with the scenery materials to the entire area. First, I sprinkle soil and dirt on the areas along the track. Then I apply the ballast and spread it evenly with a soft brush.

Before wetting the area, I tap the top of the rails with the brush shaft. The vibration pushes spilled ballast down into the ties. With an eyedropper, I drizzle the ballast and soil with the wet water mixture.

I drizzle everything with a mixture of white glue and water, starting from the highest areas and working my way down to the track. Then I sprinkle some Static Grass Flock onto the surrounding hills while they are still wet (Harvest Gold and Burnt Grass from Woodland Scenics).

In the summer heat, the shallow waters of the Donner River offer an inviting spot to cool your feet or rest before continuing our hike uphill. The water is not always so calm. Logs scattered on the riverbank are evidence that the water can also be brutal. In the spring, when the snow in the mountains melts, the boulders on the banks are covered with raging water. That is hard to imagine now. Occasionally, you will see people fishing for trout here like the guy sitting under the railroad bridge.

Riverbed

Before applying any scenery materials in the riverbed, I drilled a couple of drain holes for the glue into the plywood base. Then I applied a layer of Arizona Rock & Mineral River Bottom, which is a mixture of sand and gravel.

Next, I generously spread various shades and sizes of boulders (Woodland Scenics Talus) in the river bottom and on the banks. I also sprinkled a second layer of Arizona Rock & Mineral River Bottom down the center of the river.

I soaked everything with the wet water mixture and scattered pieces of deadwood on the banks.

I applied a lot of thinned white glue to the area to make sure all of the boulders received a sufficient amount to be sealed. The excess glue drained through the holes I had drilled in the bottom of the river.

Riverbanks have more vegetation than higher areas, so I planted a lot of Woodland Scenics Fine Leaf Foliage along my river.

I cast two 5-6mm layers of polyester as water. I dyed it with a little tan Testor's Model Master paint. Be sure to work in a well-ventilated room – the fumes could be dangerous to your health. I let the first layer harden before casting the second one.

Pine trees

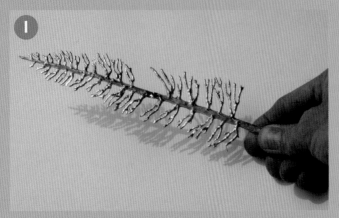

I chose Woodland Scenics pine trees with metal-style trunks for Donner River Canyon. Metal trunks keep their shape better than plastic trunks. Plastic trunks have a tendency to return to their original shape after a while.

First, I twisted the trunk like a spiral to make the branches point in all directions. Do it slowly and carefully to avoid breaking the trunk. Then I twisted all the branches into shape. I deliberately removed several branches on some of the trees to make them look a little different.

The trunks received a coat of "tree color" using Model Master 2026 Dark Drab, which is gray/brown. I airbrushed the first trees I made, but that used too much paint, so I changed procedure and brush-painted the rest of them.

I brushed some Hob-e-Tac on the branches, then tore off various pieces of foliage and attached them to the branches. And voilà – you have a fairly realistic pine tree ready to plant on your layout.

Amid tall, majestic pine trees, a freight train continues its climb through the mountains.

Vegetation on the mountain

I generously spread various types of vegetation over the area. Remember, even in areas where you don't think anything can grow, like around rock outcroppings, you'll find a surprising amount of vegetation if you look carefully. As a rule of thumb, there is an increase in vegetation growth near water, in low areas, and around rock outcroppings. In higher areas, vegetation is more sparse.

I used Clump Foliage for smaller bushes and scrubs. For larger bushes and small trees, I used Woodland Scenics Fine Leaf Foliage.

With the vegetation in place, the scenery was complete. Only a few more details had to be added, such as signals and relay sheds.

Right after I finish an area on my layout, I am thrilled with the result. I can look at it for hours and enjoy it. Then, when I look at it a couple of days later, I begin to find things that I would like to have done differently. After a month or two, I am even less satisfied with the result. It happens to me every time. I guess that is what drives me. I know I can do it better the next time.

I know you need to rest for a while now. We can sit down and wait for a train. Actually, this is a nice photo location. I have never really noticed it before. We are lucky again – here comes a train. Just what we wanted.

Trees and bushes

Planting the pine trees was easy, thanks to the brass wire I added to the bottom of the trunks. I just stuck the trees into the foam. If a tree had to be moved, I pulled it out and placed it in another location.

I used Clump Foliage for smaller bushes. I added dabs of glue to the scenery and placed pieces of Clump Foliage in the wet glue.

For larger bushes and small trees, I used Woodland Scenics Fine Leaf Foliage. This is an excellent product. Since it was introduced, I haven't used lichen at all.

We made it to Tunnel 2 and are nearing the end of our journey. I suggest we rest here for an hour before heading back down to Tunnel 1. It would be perfect if we could see a train going down this time. A train coming out of the tunnel makes for a great shot.

Final details

At last, I added final details like signals, relay sheds, and weeds. It would have been better to install the signals before ballasting the track and adding the scenery materials, but they were not available at the time. Instead, I scraped the ballast and gravel away, placed the signals, and then patched the areas again with new ballast and gravel.

The last thing to be done was a little track weathering. I dipped a stiff brush in black chalk powder and gave the center of the track a few streaks. Then the Donner River route was open for traffic.

I hope you have enjoyed Donner River Canyon as much as I have. We better get back to Tunnel 1 and our vehicle before it gets too dark. Let's make one last stop at a spot we missed on our way up. If you still have some energy, we could climb a rock and get a beautiful overhead shot down the track toward the truss bridge. Trust me, it's worth it.

The Trains

Daneville and Donner River see lots of trains: stack trains, merchandise freights, and even a few coal trains. All of these trains normally run through Daneville without stopping, except when a meet takes place. Then you can see a train stop at the Daneville siding. The only exception is the local freight, which comes every day to set out freight cars for local businesses and to pick up the empties.

This C45ACCTE is one of the few brass models in active service on my layout.

I model in the present because this is what I have experienced. My first trip to the United States was in 1992. Wide cabs were introduced to North American railroads in that period. Now they dominate the locomotive roster on all class-one railroads. It is not that I do not like the older F-units and first-generation Geeps, but I have never seen them in active duty. Well, that is not quite true. I have occasionally seen an old GP in a lash-up, but that has been the exception, not a general rule. In other words, my vision of American railroading is modern GEs and EMDs hauling double-stacks, articulated auto racks, and so forth. I find it very difficult to model something that I have not experienced.

Modeling in the present keeps me busy. Railroads receive new motive power as never before, and I try to keep pace on my railroad. By the time you read this, some of the locomotives described in this chapter could be retired or have new assignments, and new locomotives may have arrived. It is a continuous process. In addition, older freight cars are replaced with new ones all the time.

I sell my retired equipment just as the real railroads do. The amount of money I need for new investment does not allow me keep equipment I never use or can't store.

Before any new equipment hits my rails, it has received at least some weathering. The only exceptions are brass models. Unweathered brass is easier to sell and keeps a higher resale value, as most buyers are collectors who want to put them on a shelf, not to run them on a layout.

I buy brass if it is the only way I can get a specific locomotive. A few years ago, it was the only way to get models of the newest locomotives, but today, you can buy plastic models of newer locomotives soon after they are introduced on the real railroads.

Previously, I spent a good part of my hobby time kitbashing and superdetailing plastic diesels to match specific prototypes. In the last few years, out-of-the-box locomotive models have become extremely well detailed and even have the correct details for specific railroads. Now I rarely do anything to them besides a light weathering.

My locomotives also have to run smoothly. I hate to watch a jerking locomotive limping around my layout. If I can't make it run well, I simply take it out of service. Most of my older locomotive fleet, mainly composed of Athearn models, had its motors replaced with NWSL or A-Line motors. Most of my newer locomotives, like Kato, Proto 2000, Genesis, and Tower55 models, run well right out of the box.

I am a bit frustrated with my brass locomotives. They look beautiful but do not run as well as my newer plastic locomotives. One of them derails very easily. The front truck lifts its first pair of wheels when I add load to the locomotive. If I run it backwards, there is no problem. I haven't been able to figure out what is wrong with it, so I always run it backwards as a second unit in a lash-up.

The latest development on the motive power front on my layout is sound. It started when I bought two Tower55 GEVOs with sound. Suddenly, all of my other locomotives sounded a bit lame, so I started investing in sound decoders. All newly acquired locomotives must have sound. I also plan to add sound decoders to my existing fleet of locomotives.

Aging locomotives and rolling stock

When a locomotive has been in service for some time, it receives a new heavier coat of weathering. The locomotive now becomes an "older locomotive" and is assigned to low-priority freights. At some point, it will be retired, and the life cycle of the locomotive on my layout is complete.

The examples on page 69 show the same locomotive in two different stages of its life. The top photo shows how it looked during the first couple of years, with only a light coat of weathering. The bottom photo shows how it looks with a second coat of weathering applied. Many years of service will be added to the locomotive by the time it receives this additional coat of weathering.

Giving a locomotive a second weathering is quite easy and

can be done in an hour or so. Before doing anything, I clean off the dust with a soft brush. The areas I touch when handling the locomotive are carefully wiped with alcohol or thinner.

I do not disassemble a locomotive but mask windows, head-lights, number boards, and wheels. The locomotive receives a coat of a diluted light gray or sand color to simulate sun-bleached paint. Grime, soot, and rust are applied using powdered pastels. I then seal everything with a coat of Vallejo Matte Varnish.

The same technique can be used for a first weathering of a locomotive, but I usually remove the shell from the body since I have to install a decoder anyway. I also separate the wheels from the trucks in order to hand-brush them with a grimy or rusty color. As these things have already been done on a locomotive that is going to receive a second weathering, it does not need to be disassembled this time.

It can be difficult to overcome one's feelings when weather-ing a brand-new locomotive. I had mixed emotions doing it, es-pecially since I had first spent hours superdetailing my locomo-tives and giving them a "perfect" paint job. But experience has taught me that weathering is important. A weathered model

SD40-2 #3393 as it looked in its first few years, with only a light weathering.

The same engine after it received a second weathering. It has been in service for some time.

blends in with the scenery better than a non-weathered model. The next time you go train watching, notice how a brand-new car stands out. It looks unrealistically clean. The same thing applies to a model train. You can put a non-weathered car on your train and claim it is a new car. It is prototypically correct, but it does not look realistic. It might seem contradictory, but when creating a convincing illusion of the real world, you are better off modeling the average, not the extremes.

I normally do not give freight cars a second weathering. There are exceptions, but those have been caused by poorly executed weathering jobs. My freight cars show various grades of weathering, ranging from dusty to downright filthy.

I use different techniques to produce specific weathering results. Tank cars receive a thorough weathering that involve airbrushing, chalk powder, and hand-brushed oil spills. Coal hoppers receive a light coat of road grime applied with an airbrush. On the covered hoppers, I use an airbrush and chalk powder.

All cars receive a clear coat to seal the weathering. For cars that have been in service for some time, I use a flat varnish. For new cars, I use satin varnish.

The wheels on all types of cars are painted a grimy color. Finally, I brush some rust on the wheels using powdered pastels in various rust colors.

The MP15DC switcher serving Duolith Cement received a coat of weathering, complete with lots of cement dust, to match its surroundings.

Opposite page: Covered hoppers were weathered using an airbrush and chalk powder. Coal hoppers received a light coat of road grime with an airbrush. Tank cars were thoroughly weathered by airbrushing, chalk powder, and hand-brushed oil spills.

Weathering

Weathering is the key to realistic models. Even a sparsely detailed freight car can be turned into a realistic model with some weathering. I have developed a simple and quick technique for weathering my freight cars. On the following pages, you'll see the steps in weathering three types of freight cars. The boxcar and hopper are both from Athearn Genesis. The tank car is from InterMountain.

Weathering freight cars step by step

Some freight cars have patched areas. To re-create that, I place small pieces of masking tape on the sides of the boxcar. When the color of the boxcar is toned down, the patched areas will stand out.

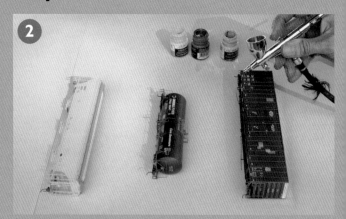

To tone down the freight cars' colors, I spray them with light coats of Model Master Sand and Light Gray thinned to almost a wash. That fades the original color but still leaves the lettering visible.

After the fading process, I remove the masking tape from the patched areas. If you want a newly patched car, just keep the masking tape on the car until the weathering is complete.

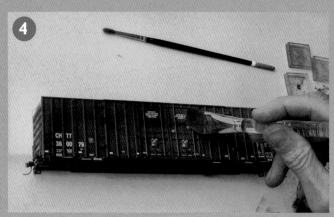

The sides and ends receive vertical streaks of brown and black powder. I work from the top to the bottom.

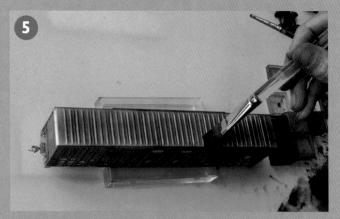

The light overspray of thinned Model Master paint leaves a flat surface suitable for chalk powder. I apply rust, brown, and black chalk powder to the boxcar roof using a soft brush.

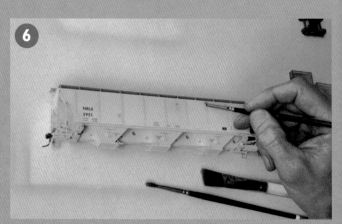

The hopper also receives chalk powder. First, I give the seams and edges a little rust using a small, hard brush.

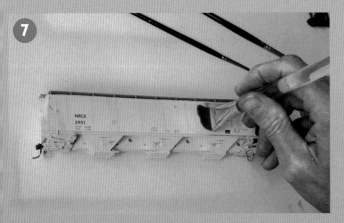

7

Then I give the entire hopper vertical streaks of brown and black chalk powder using the soft brush. Be careful not to overdo this. The chalks are much more visible on the hopper's light surface than on the boxcar's dark surface.

8

The tank car gets the same treatment, starting with a small, hard brush and some rust at the seams. I add some black powder around the dome area to simulate dirt sticking to spilled oil.

9

The entire tank car receives a good coating of brown and black powder. I start on the top of the tank and brush down the sides. The ends get their share as well.

10

All cars then receive a coat of Model Master Dark Skin Tone along the lower areas and the undersides of the cars to simulate the road grime they pick up during service. I seal everything with a coat of Vallejo Flat Clear.

11

I make jigs from thin styrene sheets to hold the trucks and cover the wheels for airbrushing. I spray the trucks with a mix of Model Master Dark Skin Tone and black.

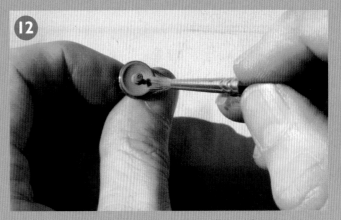

12

The wheels have to be weathered too. First, I brush-paint them with Model Master Dark Skin Tone. Then I give them some rust color using chalk powder.

The unit coal train hauled by two Kato C44ACCTEs is one of the heaviest trains seen on the Daneville subdivision.

Adding extra details to locomotives

I want my locomotives to be as accurate as possible without getting into "rivet counting." I have three different versions of the UP C44AC represented on my layout. The C44ACCTE is the newest version of the C44AC. In earlier versions, I had to do quite a detailing job to make them accurate. They started out as undecorated Athearn models. In the latest version, the C44ACCTE (based on Kato's AC4400CW), I only had to make minor changes to match the prototype (see opposite page).

The level of details on locomotive models gets better and better, so now I run several of my latest locomotive purchases right out of the box, except for some weathering.

My railroad is, of course, concerned about the environment, so the new GEVOs (C45ACCTE) can be seen around Daneville and Donner River, and soon EMD's counterpart, the SD70ACe, will be seen too.

That means I must let go of some of my older engines. Hopefully, they will find new assignments on other layouts around the world.

I normally do not add extra details to freight cars, but there are exceptions, such as this RailPower Products 56' stack car.

UP C44ACCTE details

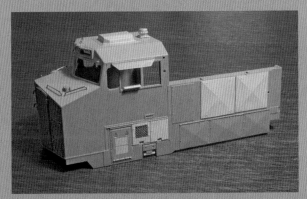

A few details were needed to turn my KATO AC-4400CWs into UP C44ACCTEs. New X-panels for the inverter cabinet and the panel on the side of the cab were made from .005" styrene. The grilles next to the new panel on the cab are filled with putty. Cab armrests are L-shaped styrene strips. The GPS dome on the roof is from Details West.

The KATOs lacked a one important detail: the brake chain on the left side of the rear truck. It was fairly simple to make eye brackets and an anchor for the brake chain from styrene bits and brass wire.

Operating my layout

I must confess that operation does not thrill me. I enjoy watching my trains roll through the scenery. Watching a long merchandise freight or stack train slowly roll by is more than enough operation for me. It is a kind of railfanning on my own layout.

However, I still planned for some operation possibilities on my layout because you never know if that part of the hobby will become more appealing in the future. I also have friends who value operations. In spite of the relatively few tracks on my layout, a modest operating session involving three to four people can take place.

My layout is DCC-operated, which allows much more opportunity than if I operated my layout using conventional DC. For example, I programmed acceleration and deceleration delay into all locomotives to make it more challenging and prototypical to operate the trains. The run-through freights take 3-4 feet to stop if they are running in speed step 18 (maximum speed being step 28). The switcher takes only 20 inches to stop from speed step 18. You really have to think ahead when operating the trains.

The local switchers

Parked down by the old Daneville depot are a couple of switchers. Their duty is to collect and distribute freight cars to the rail-served businesses in Daneville. Certainly, operating these switchers is the most challenging job on my layout.

Two rail-served businesses are situated along Daneville Road: the warehouse, which usually receives boxcars and occasionally flatcars, and, farther down the road, the plastic pellet transfer silos. All you see there are hoppers. At the other end of town, the lumber and building-supply business sees both flatcars and boxcars. Outside town, at Duolith Cement, the switchers pick up the full cement cars and set out empties. All cars are moved to the Daneville siding to be picked up later by the local freight.

The local freight leaves the cars for Daneville on the passing siding. It is the local switcher's job to move these cars to the other siding as soon as possible to avoid blocking the main line. When the cars are safely parked on the siding, the engineer checks which cars go where and plans a distribution schedule.

My son likes to operate the local switchers in Daneville. He is not particularly interested in my trains, but for some reason, he likes to operate the switchers. It takes him an about an hour to distribute and collect cars to and from the rail-served businesses in Daneville. I normally act as the switchman in these sessions, aligning the switches and uncoupling the cars.

The local switchers are on the move to pick up a car from the warehouse.

An empty boxcar at the lumberyard also has to be picked up.

All of the collected cars are set out on the siding to be picked up later by the local freight.

A typical mixed freight rolls through Daneville on a hot summer day. The high rate of trains on the Daneville subdivision makes the local switch crew's job a real challenge.

The run-through trains

The run-through trains are between 25 and 30 cars long, depending on the individual car lengths. The passing siding at Daneville sets the standard for train lengths on my layout. I have four run-through trains stored in my staging area under Daneville: two mixed freights, a stacker, and a coal train.

The run-throughs stop at Daneville if they have to meet another train, which they often do. It is nice to watch a train come to a stop at the siding and then be passed by another train. The best moment is when the stopped train gets a green light and slowly starts to move, made possible by the deceleration delay I programmed into my decoders.

In spite of the 2.6 percent grades, I can run my trains with only two engines. They struggle but manage to pull 25 to 30 cars up the grades. I sometimes add an extra engine to a lash-up because I like to see a train with more than two engines in front. Unfortunately, an extra engine takes up space, so I have to make the train a car or two shorter to make it fit the passing siding at Daneville. A shorter train does not really justify three engines, but I can always claim it is heavily loaded if anybody asks.

To me, a train with various types of freight cars is the most enjoyable kind of train to watch. I have two mixed freights. My trains are made up of boxcars, hoppers, tank cars, flatcars, a few gondolas, and an auto rack or two.

UP 8525 SD90MAC-H is a brass model from Overland Models. I painted this model myself, along with most of my brass locomotives and many of my plastic locomotives.

If I had to choose a favorite type of car, it would have to be the boxcar; to be even more specific, a modern 60-foot boxcar. Fortunately, Athearn offers a nice model of this boxcar in its Genesis line, and I have been a good customer.

I also have a stack train. It is impressive to watch a string of double-stacks roll through Daneville or Donner River Canyon. Most of my stack cars are from Walthers, and with a little weathering, they look reasonably good. One day, I hope a manufacturer will introduce a stack car with the same high level of detail as on the Genesis cars. I have made a few very detailed stack cars using A-line and RailPower Products kits, but it is very time-consuming. It takes me forever to build a complete stack train.

The last run-through train in my staging area is a 30-car coal train. During a trip to Nebraska, I really developed a taste for coal trains. Every five minutes, a train passed by, and half of them were coal trains. I got so spoiled that I did not even turn my head when a train blew its horn. There were just so many trains.

Many of the coal trains I saw had two locomotives in front and one in the rear of the train. I tried that on my layout but stopped because it caused too many problems. The pushing locomotive sometimes stalled because of dirty track, and it is not hard to guess what happens to a string of coal cars with two powerful engines pulling in front and a stalled pusher in back. And, of course, it always happens on a curve.

This BNSF mixed freight is pulled by a Kato SD70MAC and a repowered and detailed Athearn C44-9W.

The BNSF

BNSF has trackage rights in Daneville and Donner River. My favorite paint scheme of all time is the red-and-silver Santa Fe warbonnet. My old layout had 80 percent Santa Fe and 20 percent Southern Pacific trains.

The red-and-silver Santa Fe became my favorite train the minute I saw one for the first time in 1992. Sadly, they have nearly disappeared because of the merger with Burlington Northern. The few still around are in very bad shape.

In the last year of my old layout's existence, I started buying UP locomotives after the UP purchased the SP. I liked their gray-and-yellow paint scheme, so they became my favorite after the Santa Fe had gone.

In case the BNSF someday goes back to the red-and-silver warbonnet paint scheme, I have decided to give them trackage rights on my layout. As long as it sticks to its generic Great Northern paint scheme, the BNSF will only play a secondary role on my layout. But the day the warbonnets return, they will be equally represented on Daneville and Donner River. For now, I have only one BNSF train running on my layout: one of the two mixed freights running through Daneville and Donner River Canyon.

The local has stopped on the passing siding at Daneville to set out empty cement hoppers for Duolith Cement, boxcars for the lumberyard and the warehouse, and a hopper for the plastic pellet transfer. After that, it will pick up the freight cars on the siding to the right.

The local

The local comes through every day. It typically consists of two boxcars, one for the warehouse and one for the lumber and building-supply business, a hopper for the plastic pellet transfer, cement hoppers, and a coal hopper for the cement plant. Besides these cars, the local normally has three or four more cars that have fictional destinations other than Daneville.

The local leaves the cars for Daneville on the passing siding before it moves to the other track to pick up the cars the local switchers have parked on the siding. When the local has left, the local switchers move the cars to the other siding.

Maybe it doesn't sound like much, but it can easily take an hour to complete the task because you have to fit your moves in between the run-through trains, and the main line can be pretty busy.

Local switchers from Daneville collect full cement hoppers and move them to the Daneville siding. There they will be picked up by the local freight that comes once a day.

Switching at Duolith Cement

Duolith Cement is the center of operations on my layout. It is the largest industry there and has its own yard.

The cement plant has its own assigned switcher. It never leaves the plant, and its job is to move cement cars to and from the filling facility and move the coal hopper to the unloading pit.

The local UP switchers set out the cars for the cement plant on the arrival track. Then it is the company switcher's job to see that the empty cement hoppers are filled and moved to the departure track, where they will be picked up again by the local UP switcher.

The cement plant has its own control panel for operating the switches on the property. Operating the Duolith switcher is a full-time job for one person during an operating session.

Right: The company switcher picks up a full cement hopper and will move it to the departure track.

Below: The switch crew picks up an empty hopper and will move it to the filling facility.

The latest additions to my locomotive fleet, these two Tower55 GEVOs are the first sound-equipped locomotives I have.

Epilogue

A model railroad consists of more than just track, scenery, buildings, and trains. Things like benchwork, the operating system, and lighting are just as important.

Operation possibilities, scenery, and aisles are three crucial elements of a model railroad. Operation possibilities are defined by the track plan. The amount of scenery is based on how much space the track plan allows. The width of the aisles determines how comfortable they are.

It would be easy to make a dream layout if you had unlimited space and the time to build it. However, most of us have to settle with more modest conditions, such as a spare bedroom or garage and limited time. So the major challenge is to arrive at the best possible compromise, and that will always be a personal decision.

My previous layout contained a lot of scenery, which I liked, but it did not offer much in the way of operation possibilities. The aisles were also too narrow, which made operations uncomfortable.

With my previous layout in mind, my priorities were, in order of importance: nice scenery, comfortable aisles, and operation possibilities. The one compromise that was hard for me to accept was a duckunder, but there was no way I could avoid it. I hate duckunders, but I decided that I could live with one because all operations take place in Daneville. That means you don't have to pass the duckunder during an operating session.

With an 11' x 22' train room, it was not possible for me to accurately represent any prototypical areas, so I made a generic plan inspired by my favorite train places in California.

The two different types of scenery on my layout – the desert scene based on Mojave, Calif., and a mountain area such as Feather River or Donner Pass – are far apart in the real world. I had to figure out how to separate these two types of scenery on my layout. My idea was that when viewing the desert scene, you would not see the mountain scene, and visa versa.

I developed a simple track plan. Basically, it is a single track starting and ending in a hidden staging. A passing siding and various spurs to railroad-served businesses provide the operation possibilities.

I wanted my aisles to be wide enough so two people could pass. Then several people could participate in an operating session without crowding the aisles.

Framing the layout

Any layout looks more appealing with a valance and a fascia defining the edges and framing the scenes.

The only light source in my train room comes from a series of fluorescent lamps mounted behind the valance. That way, the viewer's attention is drawn to the layout scenes.

I made the valance and fascia from ⅛" Masonite sheets. The valance was the very first thing I installed on my layout, and it is much easier to do before the layout is built. This allowed me to install the fluorescent lamps without having to climb on top

of my layout, and so I had excellent light to work with when I constructed the benchwork and the layout itself.

I drew the contours of my layout onto the ceiling with chalk. I screwed 1" x 1" wood strips to the ceiling along the chalk line. Then I attached the valance to the wood strips with screws. An additional set of wood strips was glued to the back of the valance 1" from the lower edge to prevent it from bulging. I painted the back of the valance white to better reflect the light from the fluorescent lamps.

The fascia was made after the benchwork was finished but before any of the scenery was started. Using only my imagination, I drew the contour of the scenery on the fascia. I made sure there were variations in the height and depth of the scenery. Remember that no natural terrain, not even a flat-looking desert, is completely level. Finally, I used a jigsaw to cut out the scenery contours.

The fascia covers the hidden staging yard under Daneville except in one place. I made a cutout in the fascia for a workbench, which also allows access to the staging.

I do not use the workbench for larger modeling jobs. It is just for minor repairs, wheel cleaning, etc. On the staging, there is a stub-end track ending in a re-railer that I use for getting the repaired rolling stock back on the track.

Benchwork

I planned for a lightweight construction. In addition to using foam insulation board for the terrain, I also used it in the construction. Foam insulation board is light and very rigid, and when

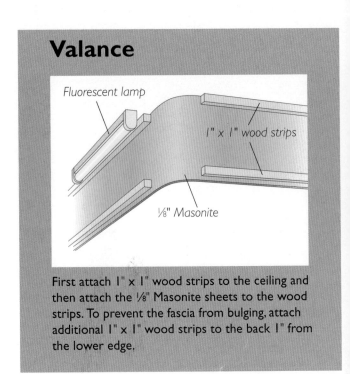

Valance

Fluorescent lamp

1" x 1" *wood strips*

⅛" *Masonite*

First attach 1" x 1" wood strips to the ceiling and then attach the ⅛" Masonite sheets to the wood strips. To prevent the fascia from bulging, attach additional 1" x 1" wood strips to the back 1" from the lower edge.

The valance and fascia define the edges of the layout and frame the scenes.

glued to the benchwork, it makes the entire construction more stable.

I did not want any legs resting on the floor. The open space under the layout makes the aisles feel wider than they really are, which is a great advantage when modeling in a limited space. Along the walls, I made a shelf-like frame from 1 x 2s (see drawings on page 89).

The freestanding section was built on 2" x 2" floor-to-ceiling wood posts (see drawings). All joints were glued and screwed together. The entire construction was surprisingly rigid, even though I didn't use any L-girders. I used ⅛" Masonite for the backdrop, cutting wide strips from sheets of Masonite in various heights. The top edge of the backdrop was to be the same height from the floor all the way around the layout. The individual heights of the strips depended on the actual layout height.

Along the wall, I mounted the Masonite strips on ½" x 2" vertical supports with screws. I let the backdrop curve around the corners to hide the fact that the layout is square.

I filled all screwheads and joints with plaster and sanded them smooth. Then I gave the entire backdrop a coat of flat white to serve as a base, which is necessary to control the colors of the sky when it is painted later.

I cut out the sub-roadbed from sheets of plywood. On my layout plan, I estimated 36" minimum radius curves on the main

I drew the contour of the scenery on the fascia …

… and cut out the scenery contours with a jigsaw.

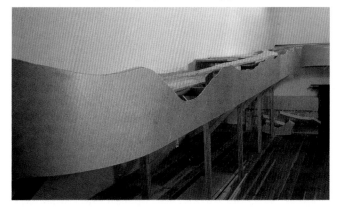

No legs rest on the floor on the right side of my layout. The freestanding section was built on floor-to-ceiling wood posts. The open space under the layout makes the aisles feel wider than they really are.

line and a maximum grade of 2.5 percent. The easements took up more space than expected, so I settled for 33" radius curves. I also had to compromise on the grades. My steepest grade ended up at 2.6 percent.

I found that the easiest way to make sure that the sub-roadbed was level was to mount the risers to the plywood sub-roadbed before attaching them to the benchwork. First, I clamped a riser to the benchwork. I then added some glue to the top of it and mounted the plywood sub-roadbed with a screw. I released the clamp and twisted it until the sub-roadbed was completely level.

I tested it by placing a carpenter's level across the top of the sub-roadbed. I then attached the riser to the benchwork with a screw.

I made an inexpensive tool for checking the grades. I took a 1" × 2" board, one meter long, and attached a screw to one end. If I wanted a 2.6 percent grade, I simply screwed the screw until the head was sticking out 2.6mm.

Then I placed it on the sub-roadbed, resting it on the screw on one end and placing a carpenter's level on top of it. When the bubble balanced, the grade was exactly 2.6 percent. I screwed the 1/8" Masonite fascia to the benchwork, drew the contour of the landscape with a pencil, and cut it out with a jigsaw.

My job as a model railroad carpenter was finally over. Between you and me, this type of work is not what I enjoy most.

The workbench under Daneville allows access to the hidden staging yard.

Benchwork

1

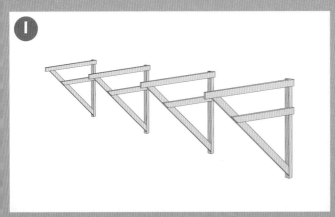

Support brackets for the hidden staging and Daneville are made from 1 x 2s screwed to the wall.

2

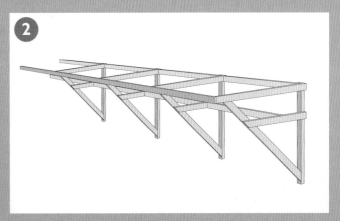

Additional 1 x 2s are placed between the brackets and along the edge.

3

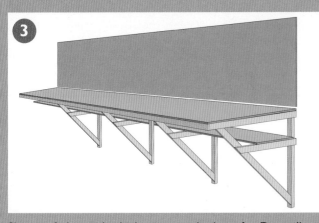

Sheets of plywood, which serve as the base for Daneville and for the hidden staging yard, are screwed to the frame. Sheets of Masonite for the backdrop are mounted to the walls on vertical ½" x 2" wood supports.

4

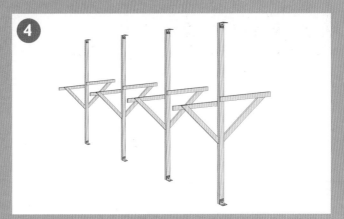

The freestanding section of my layout is comprised of 2" x 2" wood posts mounted to the floor and ceiling with metal brackets and screws. Supports for the sub-roadbed risers are made from 1 x 2s.

5

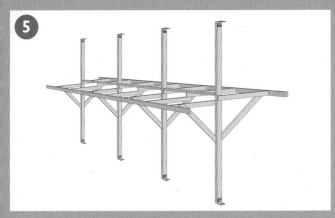

1 x 2s are attached between the posts and along the edge. The left side is lower because it is the lowest scenery point on the layout, the Donner River.

6

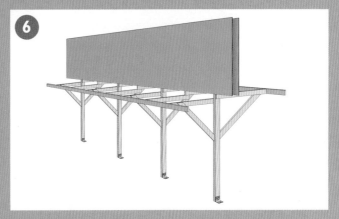

Masonite sheets for the backdrop are mounted back to back on the posts.

LEDs indicate the switch positions of the panel that serves the hidden staging.

Control system

I use DCC on my layout. To me, there is no alternative. You can operate your trains in a far more realistic manner with DCC than on a conventional layout. Wiring is also much simpler. My command station and most of my decoders are from Lenz.

I haven't figured out how my signal system will be wired. The signals and Dual Block Occupancy Detectors from Lenz are installed, and the track is divided into blocks. I hope some kind of computer-controlled system can be developed. I plan to outsource this task, since my knowledge of this subject is very limited.

All switches are powered by Tortoise switch machines, and the turnouts are controlled by toggle switches. I have three control panels: one covering the staging yard, one covering Daneville, and one for the cement plant. I made my control panels from sheets of aluminum.

The panel serving the hidden staging has LEDs that indicate the position of the switches. The panels controlling Daneville and the cement plant do not have LEDs, since all of these turnouts are visible.

Layout at a glance

Scale: HO (1:87)

Size: 11' x 22'

Prototype: Union Pacific and Burlington Northern Santa Fe

Period: Present

Locale: California

Length of mainline run: 59' (excluding staging)

Layout height: 50" to 58"

Benchwork: Wood

Roadbed: Cork

Track: Flextrack, codes 83 (main), 70 (sidings), and 55 (spurs)

Turnouts: No. 8 (main) and no. 6 sidings and yards

Minimum radius: 33"

Maximum grade: 2.6 percent

Scenery: Extruded foam insulation board

Control: Lenz Digital Command Control

Track plan

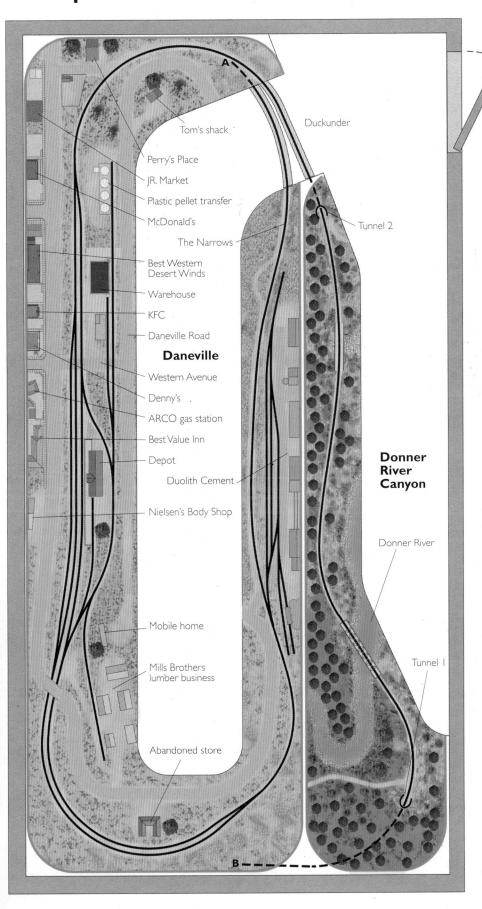

- Tom's shack
- Perry's Place
- JR. Market
- Plastic pellet transfer
- McDonald's
- The Narrows
- Best Western Desert Winds
- Warehouse
- KFC
- Daneville Road
- **Daneville**
- Western Avenue
- Denny's
- ARCO gas station
- Best Value Inn
- Depot
- Duolith Cement
- Nielsen's Body Shop
- Mobile home
- Mills Brothers lumber business
- Abandoned store

Duckunder

Tunnel 2

Donner River Canyon

Donner River

Tunnel 1

A

B

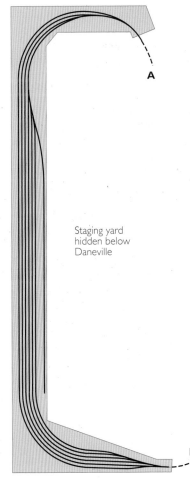

A

Staging yard hidden below Daneville

B

List of materials used on Daneville & Donner River

Basic terrain

½" Plywood (sub-roadbed)
Foam insulation board
Common water-base earth-colored paint
Sand

Woodland Scenics (www.woodlandscenics.com)

ST1444	Foam Tack Glue (or construction glue)
ST1447	Foam Putty

Track

7mm Sheets of cork Flooring cut in 17mm strips (main lines)
4mm Sheets of cork Flooring cut in 17mm strips (main lines)

Micro Engineering

10104	Code 83 Flex Track (main line)
10105	Code 83 Flex Track with Concrete Ties (main lines)
11101	Code 83 Bridge Track
10106	Code 70 Flex Track (sidings)
10108	Code 55 Flex Track (spurs)
14705	Code 83 #6 Turnout - Left Hand
14706	Code 83 #6 Turnout - Right Hand
14805	Code 70 #6 Turnout - Left Hand
14806	Code 70 #6 Turnout - Right Hand
30104	Spikes - Medium
30106	Spikes - Small
26055	Rail Joiners - Code 55
26070	Rail Joiners - Code 70
26083	Rail Joiners - Code 83

Central Valley Model Works (www.cvmw.com)

2881	Turnout Kit #8 - Left Hand
2882	Turnout Kit #8 - Right Hand

Desert scenery (Daneville)

Arizona Rock & Mineral (www.rrscenery.com)

110-03	Low Desert Soil
1203	Cajon Sand Stone - Sand and Gravel
1205	Cajon Sand Stone - Rip-Rap (medium)
1207	Cajon Sand Stone - Rip-Rap (large)

Woodland Scenics (www.woodlandscenics.com)

C1230	Rock Mold - Outcroppings
C1231	Rock Mold - Surface Rocks
C1201	Lightweight Hydrocal
C1218	Liquid Pigment - Stone Gray
C1222	Liquid Pigment - Burnt Umber
C1223	Liquid Pigment - Yellow Ocher
FC144	Bushes - Olive Green
FC181	Clump-Foliage - Burnt Grass
FG171	Field Grass - Natural Straw
FG172	Field Grass - Harvest Gold
FL632	Static Flock Grass - Harvest Gold
T1362	Coarse Turf - Burnt Grass
F1132	Fine-Leaf Foliage - Light Green
F1133	Fine-Leaf Foliage - Olive Green

Hart Of The South Models (www.hartofthesouth.com)

5-SP-2	5" Sabal Palmetto - Palm Tree Kit
30-1-SP	1" Sabal Palmetto - Fronds Only

Desert scenery (The Narrows)

Arizona Rock & Mineral (www.rrscenery.com)

110-03	Low Desert Soil
107-03	High Desert Soil
1205	Cajon Sand Stone - Rip-Rap (medium)

Woodland Scenics (www.woodlandscenics.com)

C1230	Rock Mold - Outcroppings
C1234	Rock Mold - Random Rock
C1241	Rock Mold - Layered Rock
C1201	Lightweight Hydrocal
C1218	Liquid Pigment - Stone Gray
C1220	Liquid Pigment - Black
C1221	Liquid Pigment - Raw Umber
C1222	Liquid Pigment - Burnt Umber
C1223	Liquid Pigment - Yellow Ocher
FC144	Bushes - Olive Green
FC181	Clump-Foliage - Burnt Grass
FG171	Field Grass - Natural Straw
FG172	Field Grass - Harvest Gold
FL632	Static Flock Grass - Harvest Gold
T1362	Coarse Turf - Burnt Grass
C1275	Talus, Medium - Brown

F1132   Fine-Leaf Foliage - Light Green
F1133   Fine-Leaf Foliage - Olive Green

Mountain scenery (Donner River)

Arizona Rock & Mineral (www.rrscenery.com)

107-03	High Desert Soil
118-03	Oak Creek Orange - Sand and Gravel
1203	Cajon Sand Stone - Sand and Gravel
1205	Cajon Sand Stone - Rip-Rap (medium)
1020	Earth
138-04	River Bottom Mix - Rock, Sand and Powder

Woodland Scenics (www.woodlandscenics.com)

C1230	Rock Mold - Outcroppings
C1231	Rock Mold - Surface Rocks
C1234	Rock Mold - Random Rock
C1240	Rock Mold - Rock Mass
C1241	Rock Mold - Layered Rock
C1244	Rock Mold - Facet Rock
C1201	Lightweight Hydrocal
C1218	Liquid Pigment - Stone Gray
C1219	Liquid Pigment - Slate Gray
C1220	Liquid Pigment - Black
C1221	Liquid Pigment - Raw Umber
C1222	Liquid Pigment - Burnt Umber
FC181	Clump-Foliage - Burnt Grass
FC182	Clump-Foliage - Light Green
FG171	Field Grass - Natural Straw
FG172	Field Grass - Harvest Gold
FL632	Static Flock Grass - Harvest Gold
FL633	Static Flock Grass - Burnt Grass
T1362	Coarse Turf - Burnt Grass
F1131	Fine-Leaf Foliage - Medium Green
F1132	Fine-Leaf Foliage - Light Green
F1133	Fine-Leaf Foliage - Olive Green
C1270	Talus, fine - Buff
C1274	Talus, fine - Brown
C1271	Talus, medium - Buff
C1275	Talus, medium - Brown
C1272	Talus, coarse - Buff
C1276	Talus, coarse - Brown
TK23	Large Tree Kits - Pine Tree

Tunnels

Woodland Scenics (www.woodlandscenics.com)

C1252	Tunnel Portal - Concrete Single Track
C1258	Retaining Walls - Concrete
C1250	Tunnel Liner Form
C1201	Lightweight Hydrocal
C1218	Liquid Pigment - Stone Gray
C1219	Liquid Pigment - Slate Gray
C1220	Liquid Pigment - Black

Roads

Woodland Scenics (www.woodlandscenics.com)

ST1452	Smooth-It - Plaster
ST1455	Paving Tape - Adhesive-backed foam tape

Testors Model Master Paint

1730	Flat Gull Gray

Pikestuff (www.rixproducts.com)

541-0013	Highway Guardrails

Trackside details

Details West (www.detailswest.com)

GT-916	Ground Throw Switch Stand
SM-903	Switch Control - Motor and Tie Mount
CS-913	Crossing Signal

Grant Line

5910	Standard Relay House

N.J. International (www.njinternational.com)

525-1172	Crossing Gates

Rix Products (www.rixproducts.com)

628-0030	Telephone Poles
628-0035	Clear Crossarms for Telephone Poles

Berkshire Junction (www.bershirejunction.com)

1471HB	EZ Line, elastic string for telephone lines
1471OB	EZ Line, elastic string for electric lines

Buildings

Walthers (www.walthers.com)
933-3081 Plastic Pellet Transfer - Silos
933-3082 Mills Bros. Lumber - Lumber Industry
933-3086 Blue Star Ready Mix - Truck Loading Facility
933-3098 Valley Cement - Cement Plant

Laserkit (www.laserkit.com)
801   Santa Fe Depot #3 (Daneville Depot)
126   Mrs. Williams House (Perry's Place)
705   Sonny's Shack (Tom's Place)

Great West Models Inc.
110   One-Story Office/Warehouse

Pikestuff (www.rixproducts.com)
541-16   Yard Office
541-10   Distrib. Center (Nielsen's Body Shop)

NuComp Miniatures (www.nucompinc.com)
871005   Mobile Home #1

Bridges

Walthers (www.walthers.com)
933-3185 Single-Track Truss Bridge
933-1040 Abutments
933-1042 Abutment Wings

Central Valley Model Works (www.cvmw.com)
1903   Single-Track Plate Girder Bridge

Rix Products (www.rixproducts.com)
628-111   Modern Highway Overpass

Signals

Sunrise Enterprises (www.sunrisenterprises.com)
111002   Target Signal - Single
111052   Target Signal - Dual

MicroScale Models (www.microscale.ch)
901-002-S UP Signal - Single Head
902-002-S UP Signal - Dual Head

Miscellaneous

Common White Glue (for gluing ground cover, ballast, etc.)
Rubbing Alcohol (for "wet water")

Index

Add realistic details to your next layout!

Realistic Model Railroad Design

Model Railroader magazine author Tony Koester shows you how to make creative, plausible choices for the concept and construction of your next model railroad. Covers key topics like developing an entire model railroad theme, choosing a scale, integrating design elements into your track plan, and much more. 8-1/4 x 10-3/4; 96 pgs.; 150 color and 10 b&w photos; 50 illus.; softcover.

12250 • $19.95

The Model Railroader's Guide to Passenger Equipment & Operations

Even today, passenger trains represent a major part of daily operations on North American rails. This book from Andy Sperandeo, *Model Railroader* executive editor, offers insight and instructions to help modelers integrate realistic passenger trains and operations into any layout. 8-1/4 x 10-3/4; 96 pages; 130 color & 70 b&w photos; 20 illus.; softcover.

12244 • $19.95

Trackside Scenes You Can Model

Historic color and black-and-white photographs capture prototype railroad settings from all over U.S. The author details how you can realistically model each scene on your layout. Each chapter features a description of the scene including trackage, structures, operating environment, and suggested track plan. By Jim Kelly. 8-1/4 x 10-3/4; 80 pgs.; 80 color and 20 b&w photos; 25 illus.; softcover.

12234 • $18.95

Every issue includes intriguing articles that take you on a tour of the world's finest layouts and introduce you to the hobby's experts. You'll also discover a wealth of prototype data, detailed how-to instructions, product reviews, tips, techniques, and so much more! 12 issues per year

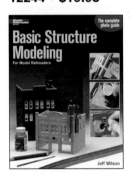

Basic Structure Modeling for Model Railroaders

Photo-driven projects demonstrate the tools, materials, and techniques used when modeling plastic or wood structures. Offers techniques for realistic finishing, including painting, weathering, sign making, interior detailing, and more. By Jeff Wilson. 8-1/4 x 10-3/4; 88 pgs.; 225 color photos; 12 illus.; softcover.

12258 • $19.95

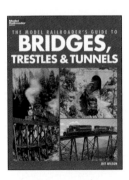

The Model Railroader's Guide to Bridges, Trestles, & Tunnels

Each chapter shows prototype examples and ways to model, paint, weather, and install them on a layout. Includes details for numerous types of bridges. Perfect for intermediate and advanced hobbyists. By Jeff Wilson. 8-1/4 x 10-3/4; 88 pgs; 75 color and 100 b&w photos; 15 illus.; softcover.

12452 • $19.95